LIVING AND NONLIVING

by Alexandria Berry

Published in the United States of America by Cherry Lake Publishing Group
Ann Arbor, Michigan
www.cherrylakepublishing.com

Reading Adviser: Beth Walker Gambro, MS, Ed., Reading Consultant, Yorkville, IL

Photo Credits:
© Nicoleta Ionescu/Shutterstock, (cartoon girl on cover and throughout book), © Iren_Geo/Shutterstock, (photo) cover; © Cassette Bleue/Shutterstock, speech bubbles throughout; © VIDYASKANDAN/Shutterstock, (elephant), © Bigzumi/Shutterstock, (ants), page 5; © xpixel/Shutterstock, (shells), ©BW Press/Shutterstock, editorial use only, (monster truck), page 6; © branislavpudar/Shutterstock, (plants), © Mogens Trolle/Shutterstock, (zebra), page 7; © Arthur Caleb Robertson/Shutterstock, (trees), © Ljupco Smokovski/Shutterstock, (people), page 9;© FrentaN/Shutterstock, (fish), © Gulzar fakir/Shutterstock, (bird), page 10; Kuttelvaserova Stuchelova/Shutterstock, (flytrap), © RM911/Shutterstock, (sunflowers), page 11; © BlueRingMedia/Shutterstock, page 12; © VectorMine/Shutterstock, page 13; © Phawat/Shutterstock, (gold), © Valentin Valkov/Shutterstock, (teddy), © Mike_O/Shutterstock,(rocks), page 14; © xiaorui/Shutterstock, (T shirts), © Terelyuk/Shutterstock, (sheep), © New Africa/Shutterstock, (paper), page 15; © Andrei Armiagov/Shutterstock, page16-17; © erskine/Shutterstock, (goat), © Barbora Polivkova/Shutterstock, (fox), page 17; © Michael Potts F1/Shutterstock, (race car, editorial use only), © Moses P/Shutterstock, (city), page 18; © PeopleImages.com - Yuri A/Shutterstock, (child), © SPF/Shutterstock, (toy cat), page 19; © Likoper/Shutterstock, (people), © Nick Greeves/Shutterstock, (whale), page 20; © wk1003mike/Shutterstock, (plants), © Engel Ching/Shutterstock, (city), page 21

Produced by bluedooreducation.com for Cherry Lake Publishing

Copyright © 2026 by Cherry Lake Publishing Group

All rights reserved. No part of this book may be reproduced or utilized in any form or by any means without written permission from the publisher.

Library of Congress Cataloging-in-Publication Data has been filed and is available at catalog.loc.gov.

Printed in the United States of America

Note from Publisher: Websites change regularly, and their future contents are outside of our control. Supervise children when conducting any recommended online searches for extended learning opportunities.

TABLE OF CONTENTS

Living or Nonliving? 4

Living Things 7

Nonliving Things 14

Let's Compare! 19

Think About It 22
Glossary 23
Find Out More 24
Index 24
About the Author 24

LIVING OR NONLIVING?

Look at the cover of this book.
Is the dog living or nonliving?

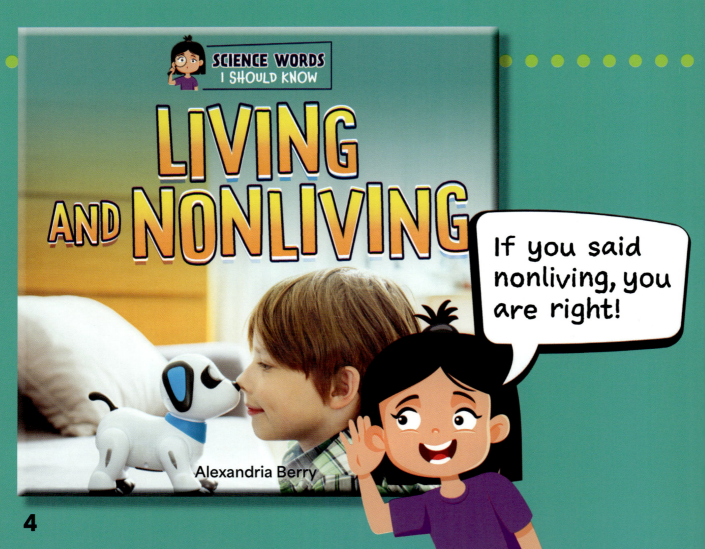

Some things are alive, like animals and plants.

Other things, like rocks or toys, are not alive.

Living things can be big, like an elephant, or small, like an ant!

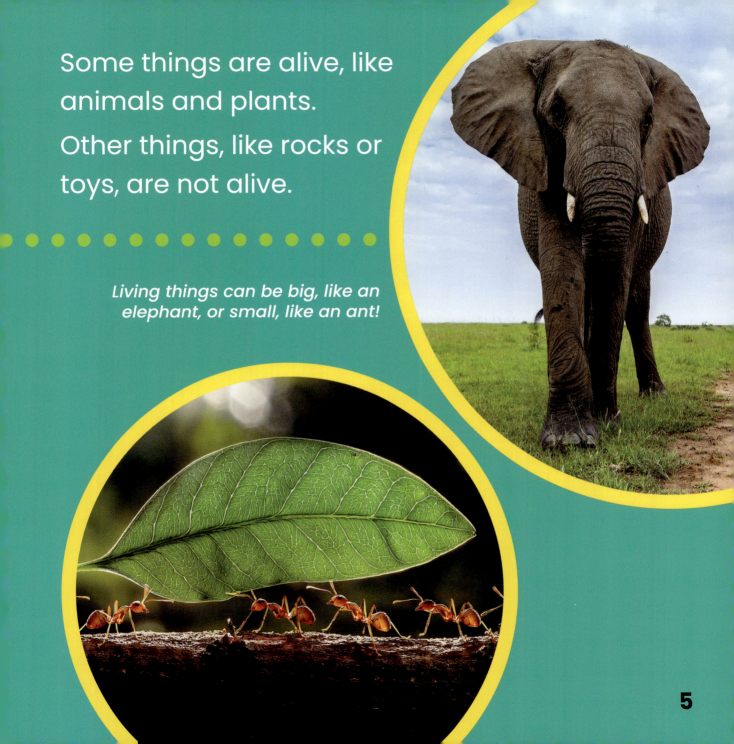

Nonliving things can be big, like a monster truck, or small, like a grain of sand.

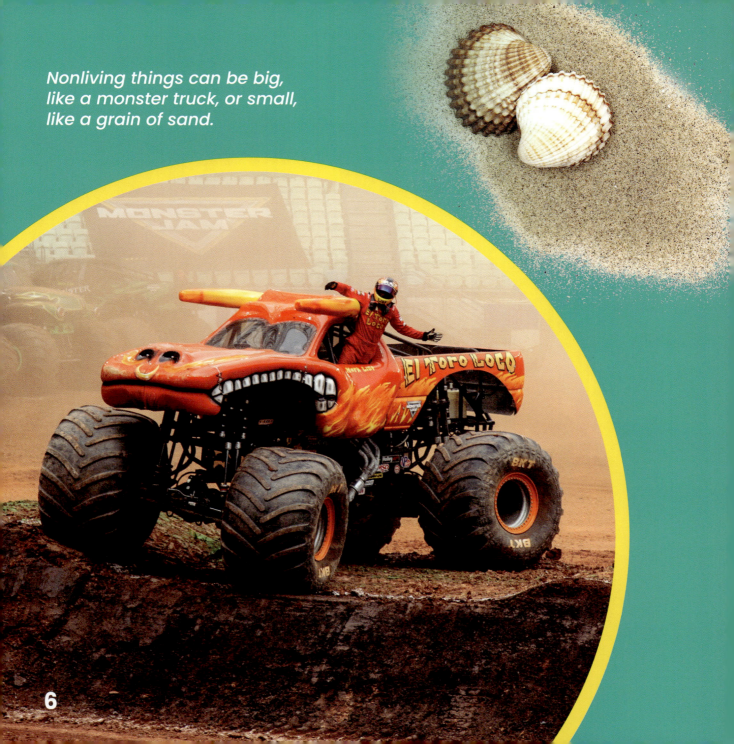

LIVING THINGS

All living things turn food into energy. They use the energy to grow and **survive**.

Plants make their own food with sunlight. Animals eat plants or other animals.

7

Living things grow.
They can get bigger over time.

Sequoia trees can grow over 300 feet (91.4 meters) tall.

Some trees can live for thousands of years.

Trees grow taller. Babies grow into adults. Everything alive can grow and change in some way.

Living things can move. They can move in many ways!

Birds fly, fish swim, and people walk or run.

Even plants move in some ways. They react to the world around them.

Movement helps living things find food, water, or safety.

A Venus flytrap closes and traps its prey.

Sunflowers turn to face the Sun!

Living things **reproduce**. They make more living things. Plants grow seeds that become new plants.

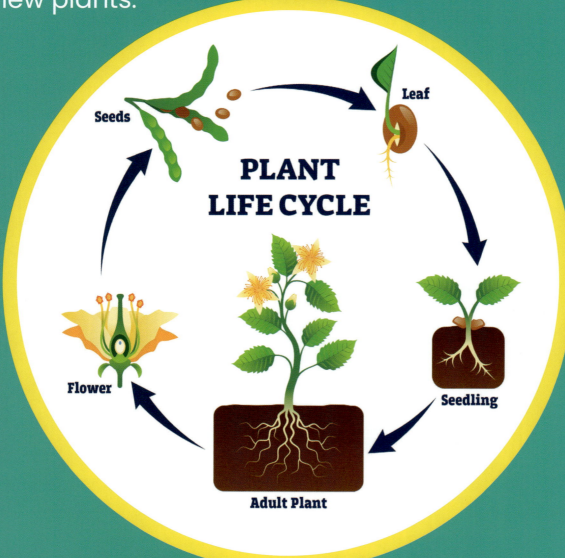

Mammals have babies. Most **reptiles** lay eggs.

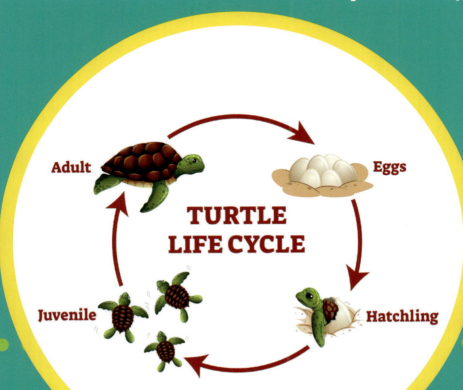

1	2	3	4
It turns food into energy.	It grows.	It moves on its own in some way.	It can reproduce.

These things mean that something is living.

NONLIVING THINGS

Nonliving things don't grow or change on their own. They don't eat food like living things do.

A shiny rock may look special, but it's not alive.

Nonliving things cannot move on their own.

Some nonliving things used to be part of something alive.

Many of your clothes, like T-shirts and jeans, start as cotton plants grown on farms.

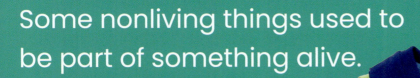

Living Beginnings

Paper comes from trees. Wool comes from sheep.

Even though they start from living things, wool and paper are not alive.

This makes them nonliving things.

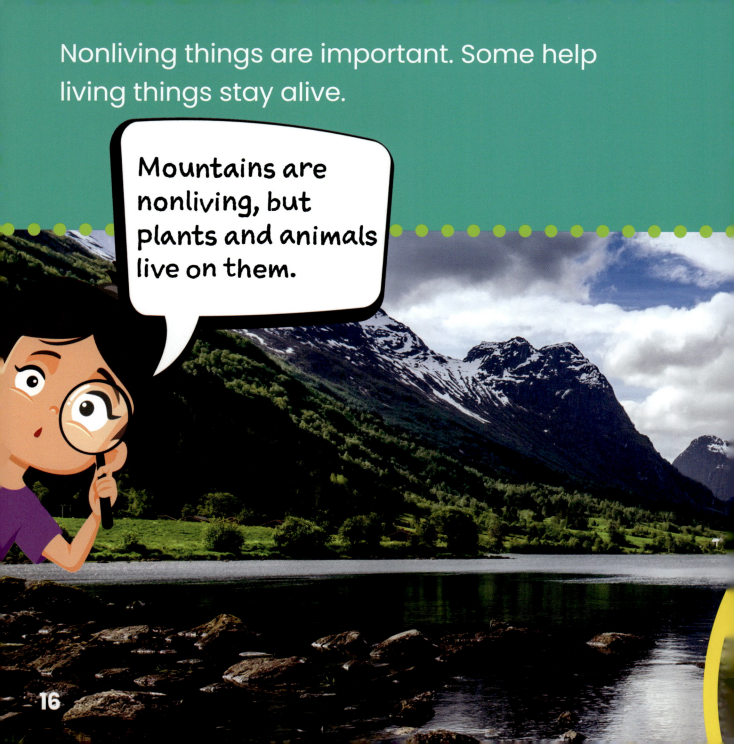

Nonliving things are important. Some help living things stay alive.

Mountains are nonliving, but plants and animals live on them.

Some nonliving things are **natural**.

Rivers, mountains, clouds, and water are natural, nonliving things.

Some mountains are homes for goats.

Water is nonliving, but it helps plants and animals stay alive.

17

Some nonliving things are **man-made**. Buildings and cars are nonliving.

buildings: BIL-dingz

LET'S COMPARE!

Living and nonliving things are very different.

Living things grow, eat, and move.

Nonliving things do not.

19

Living things **breathe** to stay alive. People and animals breathe air.

Nonliving things, like toys and chairs, don't breathe at all.

A Breath of Fresh Air
Whales are mammals. They live in water, but they come to the surface to breathe. They breathe air just like you.

Living and nonliving things are both special. Together, they make the world a wonderful place!

THINK ABOUT IT

Using what you have learned in this book, match each sentence to the correct picture.

1 This nonliving thing is made by people.

2 This living thing turns toward the Sun.

3 This nonliving thing is found in nature.

4 This living thing swims underwater.

A.

B.

C.

D.

Answers: 1C 2D 3B 4A

22

GLOSSARY

breathe (BREETH) to take in air and let it out, which living things need to do to stay alive

mammals (MAM-uhlz) animals with hair or fur that give birth to babies and feed them milk

man-made (MAN-MAYD) made by people, like houses, cars, and toys

natural (NACH-ur-uhl) things found in nature, like rivers, mountains, and trees

reproduce (REE-pruh-doos) to make more living things

reptiles (REP-tielz) scaly, cold-blooded animals that usually lay eggs

survive (sur-VIEV) to stay alive

Find Out More

Books
Dunne, Abbie. *Living or Nonliving?*, North Mankato, MN, Capstone Press: 2016

Kurtz, Kevin. *Living and Nonliving Things*. Mount Pleasant, SC, Arbordale Publishing: 2017

Websites
Search these online sources with an adult:

Living and Nonliving Things | Tiny Tap

Living Things in My Backyard | PBS

Index

air 20
animals 5, 7, 16, 17, 20
breathe 20
grow(s) 7, 8, 9, 13, 19
man-made 18
plants 5, 11, 12, 15
survive 7
water 11, 17

About the Author

Alexandria Berry is an animal lover who shares her St. Louis home with two dogs, two cats, and one corn snake. As a fifth-grade teacher, she is passionate about inspiring young minds to explore the wonders of the natural world.